M000035052

## OTHER GIFTBOOKS IN THIS SERIES

*baby boy!*    *dad*    *happy day!*
*baby girl!*    *smile*    *hope! dream!*
*friend*    *love*

Printed simultaneously in 2004 by Helen Exley Giftbooks
in Great Britain and Helen Exley Giftbooks LLC in the USA.

12 11 10 9 8 7 6 5 4 3 2 1

Illustrations © Joanna Kidney 2004
Copyright © Helen Exley 2004
Text copyright – see page 95
The moral right of the author has been asserted.

ISBN 1-86187-916-4

Edited by Helen Exley
Pictures by Joanna Kidney

Printed in China

**Helen Exley Giftbooks, 16 Chalk Hill, Watford, Herts WD19 4BG, UK.**
**Helen Exley Giftbooks LLC, 185 Main Street, Spencer MA 01562, USA.**
**www.helenexleygiftbooks.com**

A HELEN EXLEY GIFTBOOK

# mom

PICTURES BY JOANNA KIDNEY

A mother laughs our laughter,
Sheds our tears,
Returns our love,
Fears our fears.
She lives our joys,
Cares our cares,
And all our hopes and dreams
she shares.

JULIA SUMMERS

I have learned to really hear the message
my mother has given me all my life:
"I will be with you always".
As in forever,
into the eternal hereafter,
no matter what.

REBECCA WALKER,
DAUGHTER OF ALICE WALKER

An ounce of mother is worth

all the flowers in the world.

IONA ALLFORD

My mother...
the one who listened and listened
to all my drivel,
always took my side,
ready to pick up the sword
and kill the enemy next to me.
She was the person
I did my tricks for.

JOAN RIVERS, B.1933,
FROM "STILL TALKING"

All mothers are rich
when they love their children.
There are no poor mothers,
no ugly ones,
no old ones.
Their love is always
the most beautiful
of the joys.

 COUNT MAURICE MAETERLINCK
(1862–1949)

When mamma smiled,
beautiful as her face was,
it grew incomparably more lovely,
and everything around
seemed brighter.

LEO TOLSTOY (1828–1910)

The goodness of a home
is not dependent on wealth,
or spaciousness,
or beauty, or luxury.
Everything
depends on the Mother.

G.W.E. RUSSELL (1867–1935)

Most of all the other beautiful things in life
come by twos and threes,
by dozens and hundreds.
Plenty of roses, stars, sunsets, rainbows,
brothers and sisters,
aunts and cousins,
but only one mother
in the whole world.

KATE DOUGLAS WIGGIN (1856–1953)

"You are the caretaker
of the generations,
        you are the birth giver,"
the sun told the woman.
        "You will be
    the carrier
        of this universe."

BRULE SIOUX SUN CREATION MYTH

A mother is love.
That's where
you get your first taste of love.
When you are afraid,
a mother holds you.
When you have a problem,
a mother talks to you.
A mother is there.

MS. CARSON, "ST. PETERSBURG TIMES",
FLORIDA, MAY 12, 1996

That is the most crucial influence
one can have
– a loving and caring mother.
To make one feel
one is worthwhile.

BETTE DAVIS (1908–1989),
IN AN INTERVIEW BY BOZE HADLEIGH

My mom is as beautiful
as anyone can be,
well maybe not to everyone
but always to me.
Now I don't mean always by looks
because you learn all that junk
from T.V. and books.
But I mean
that she has a beauty inside.

DONNA NITTE, AGE 12

She laughs when I laugh,
she cries when I cry,
she lives when I live

I can't say more about her
except that she lives for me
and I live for her.

JOSEPHIDES PANAYIOTA, AGE 16

Thank you, Mom,
for all the dirty dishes you've washed,
the wet laundry you've hung out to dry,
the baskets of school clothes
you've sprinkled and ironed,
the lawns you've mowed
and the broken hearts and fences you've mended.
Thank you for the countless ways
you've given your love,
your wisdom, your strength...

COOKIE CURCI, FROM "WILLOW GLEN RESIDENT",
SAN JOSE WEEKLY, MAY 15, 1996

She is kind and gentle.
Sometimes
     my mother really loves me
and she looks at my face
     and smiles at me.
I go and sit by her.

BALBINDER KAUR KALSI, AGE 11

Mothers
hold the world together
when all seems
set on its destruction.

PAM BROWN, B.1928

Thank you for being there
come fire, flood or penury.

Thank you for being ready
to lend anything,
give anything
that will help us through.

PAM BROWN, B.1928

She opened my heart
to the impressions of nature;
she awakened my understanding

nd extended my horizon,

     and her precepts exerted

  an everlasting influence

     upon the course of my life.

IMMANUEL KANT (1724–1804)

My mother is like the weather
and I am just a seed.
Without the sun or the rain
I would not be able to grow into a flower,
healthy and beautiful.
Her warmth and love makes me grow.
Bigger and bigger.

LING TAI, AGE 11

# Home-made jam

from Mom is really bottled love.

H.M.E.

## *Women Know*

The way to rear up children, (to be just),
They know a simple,
merry, tender knack
Of tying sashes, fitting baby-shoes,
And stringing pretty words
that make no sense,
And kissing full sense
into empty words.

ELIZABETH BARRETT BROWNING
(1806-1861)

IT IS LOVELY TO HAVE A MAM.
Mams are lovely people
and I am going to be a lovely mother
when I grow up.
I am going to care
for my children
like my parents cared for me.

ESTELLE MORETON

Mother, I love you so.
Said the child,
I love you more than I know.
She laid her head on her mother's arm,
And the love between them kept
them warm.

STEVIE SMITH (1902–1971)

There is in all this world
no fount of deep, strong,
            deathless love,
    save that within
            a mother's heart.

FELICIA HEMANS (1793–1835)

Dear Mother.
Never listens to an argument,
never lets logic interfere
with the warm impulses of her heart.
Singing around the house,
a girl's voice still,
a bird's heart.
Capricious, unpredictable,
generous, tactless,
stubborn, unreasonable,
and lovable mother.

MAURICE WIGGIN

# Your mother

is your best friend.

DEAN, AGE 8

It is wonderful to meet
and talk over everything
and share and laugh
and understand each other's situations
as no one else can.

ANNE MORROW LINDBERGH (1906–2001)

...my mother and her teachings
were after all
the only capital
I had to start life with,
and on that capital
I have made my way.

ANDREW JACKSON

**W**ho is it that loves me
and will love me for ever
    with an affection which
no chance, no misery,
    no crime of mine can do away?
    It is you,
        my mother.

THOMAS CARLYLE (1795–1881)

She is their earth....
　　She is their food and their bed
and the extra blanket
　　when it grows cold in the night;
she is their warmth and their health
　　　　and their shelter.

KATHARINE BUTLER HATHAWAY

*A happy childhood
is one of the best gifts
that parents
have in their power
to bestow.*

R. CHOLMONDELEY

Other folks can love you,
but only your mother understands;
She works for you
– looks after you –
Loves you,
forgives you....

BARONESS VON HUTTON

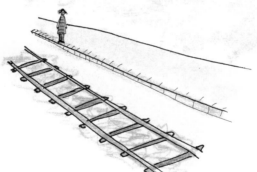

**Nothing looks
as lonely as your mom
before she sees you
coming up
the platform.**

PAM BROWN, B.1928

**Mothers need
transfusions
fairly often – phone calls**

letters, bright postcards
from the Outer Hebrides.

HEULWEN ROBERTS

Through the years, we've come to discover
that money can be lost
and property ruined.
But what Mom has so generously
given to her family
can't be damaged or destroyed.
Her love has always been
a love without conditions.

COOKIE CURCI, FROM "WILLOW GLEN RESIDENT",
SAN JOSE WEEKLY, MAY 15, 1996

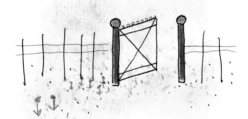

The most important thing
my mom has given me
is the belief
that anything is possible

# as long as you follow your dream.

AMMIE LUNN, FROM "LONDON FREE PRESS",
LONDON, ONTARIO, MAY 15, 1996

In later life you may have friends,
fond, dear friends,
but never will you have again
the inexpressible love and gentleness
lavished upon you,
which none but mother bestows.

THOMAS BABINGTON MACAULAY
(1800–1859)

It doesn't matter how old I get,
whenever I see anything new or splendid,
I want to call,
"Mom, come and look."

HELEN EXLEY

A mother does not realise
that she is giving her child
memories to last a lifetime.

CHARLOTTE GRAY, B.1937

You made me believe
that if I tried hard enough
I could do anything.
And so I did!

HELEN THOMSON, B.1943

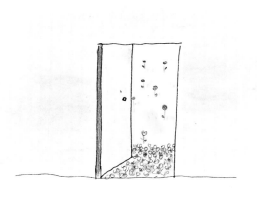

Whether we are six or sixty,
whether we see our mother every day
or every four years on Mother's Day,
we honor her,
and on some level,
we go home to her.

CAROL J. CAPERELLI,
FROM "CHICAGO TRIBUNE", MAY 12, 1996

*Of all the mums
in all the world
how marvellous
that you are mine.*

CHARLOTTE GRAY, B.1937

Thank you
for the golden days
and quiet nights.
Thank you for everything.

PAM BROWN, B.1928

My mother has always
been totally loving, totally patient,
totally understanding.
And I know that the feeling
of being loved
and cared for
will be with me my whole life.

HELEN THOMSON, B.1943

*Wherever mum is,*
*that's where*
*home is.*

FELICITY MARTIN

Helen Exley runs her own publishing company which sells giftbooks in more than seventy countries. She had always wanted to do a little book on smiles, and had been collecting the quotations for many years, but always felt that the available illustrations just weren't quite right. Then Helen fell in love with Joanna Kidney's happy, bright pictures and knew immediately they had the feel she was looking for. She asked Joanna to work on *smile*, and then to go on to contribute the art for four more books: *friend*, *happy day!*, *love* and *hope! dream!* We are now publishing five more books in this series, *dad*, *mum*, *baby boy!*, *baby girl!* and *wedding*.

Joanna Kidney lives in County Wicklow in Ireland. She juggles her time between working on various illustration projects and producing her own art for shows and exhibitions. Her whole range of greeting cards, *Joanna's Pearlies* – some of which appear in this book – won the prestigious 2001 Henries oscar for 'best fun or graphic range'.

**Helen Exley Giftbooks**
16 Chalk Hill, Watford, WD19 4BG, UK,
185 Main Street, Spencer, MA 01562, USA,
www.helenexleygiftbooks.com